Hypnotized

Don Trembath

Orca currents

ORCA BOOK PUBLISHERS

To Jen and Spyder, for all the ridiculous fun we have together.

Library and Archives Canada Cataloguing in Publication
Trembath, Don, 1963-
Hypnotized / written by Don Trembath.
(Orca currents)
ISBN 978-1-55143-707-1 (bound)
ISBN 978-1-55143-705-7 (pbk.)
I. Title. II. Series.
PS8589.R392H96 2007 jC813'.54 C2007-900249-8

Summary: Rufus and his sister's relationship changes after
he attempts to hypnotize her.

First published in the United States, 2007
Library of Congress Control Number: 2007920335

Orca Book Publishers gratefully acknowledges the support for its
publishing programs provided by the following agencies: the Government
of Canada through the Book Publishing Industry Development Program
and the Canada Council for the Arts, and the Province of British Columbia
through the BC Arts Council and the Book Publishing Tax Credit.

Cover design: Doug McCaffry
Cover photography: Getty Images

The author would like to express his sincere thanks to the
Alberta Foundation for the Arts for its generous
funding of this project.

Orca Book Publishers
PO Box 5626, Station B
Victoria, BC Canada
V8R 6S4

Orca Book Publishers
PO Box 468
Custer, WA USA
98240-0468

www.orcabook.com
Printed and bound in Canada.
Printed on 100% PCW recycled paper.
010 09 08 07 • 5 4 3 2 1

chapter one

My friend Phil wants to be a hypnotist. He's read, like, twenty books about it, and he took a course on the Internet. I'm his guinea pig. He just tried hypnotizing me again.

It didn't work.

"Maybe we need someone with a smaller brain," says Phil after pouting for half an hour. "You gotta crawl before you can walk, right?"

I ask my sister Alexa. She's fifteen, two years older than me. She's on the short side and she hates her body because she thinks she's getting fat, which she is. But now is not the time to let her know I agree with her.

"What?" she says, after I pound on her bedroom door for ten minutes.

"Take your headphones off," I say to her. The music she's playing on her iPod is so loud that I feel like taking my headphones off, and I'm not wearing any.

"What?" she says again with a frown.

I repeat myself, only this time, I scream so loud that the neighbor's dog two doors down starts barking.

Alexa removes her headphones. "This better be good."

"We need someone with a small brain for Phil to practice hypnosis on," I say to her.

Alexa's not nearly as sensitive about her brain as she is about her body.

"What, he couldn't find yours at all?" She thinks she's so funny.

"Just say yes, Alexa," I say to her. "Spare us the comedy."

She looks at Phil. "You're a hypnotist? Since when?"

Phil shrugs and stares at his feet. "I sorta am, yeah. Kinda. You know. A little bit," he says. Way to inspire confidence, Phil. She has to go for it now. How could she possibly say no?

"No," she says, "go look somewhere else. And don't pound on my door again."

"Aww come on," I say to her. "It'll be fun."

"I'm going back into my bedroom to clip my toenails. That's fun compared to hanging out with you schmucks." She starts to close her door.

"We'll pay you ten bucks," blurts Phil, as a last resort.

The door whips open. "Where do I sit?" says Alexa.

We go downstairs. Phil gets her a chair, and I give her all the instructions she needs. "Just sit here and watch the gold medal Phil has in his hand."

"Where'd you two losers get a gold medal from?" she says.

Alexa is a very nice person—always positive and encouraging.

"You can buy them at the dollar store," says Phil. He is way too honest sometimes. I would have told her we won it in an Ultimate Warrior Fighting tournament.

Alexa smirks and raises an eyebrow. Then she slouches in her chair, crosses her arms and stares as Phil goes through his routine.

I watch her to see if any changes take place.

"Stop looking at me." She turns away from Phil, which she's not supposed to do, and looks at me.

"Hey, what are you doing?" I say, leaping out of my chair. I can get pretty excited.

"What do you mean, what am I doing? Stop looking at me. God, you think I want that?"

"I'm watching to see if you're hypnotized," I explain to her.

"I'll tell you if I'm hypnotized. Stop staring at me. You're freaking me out."

"I'm freaking you out? Have you seen yourself lately?" I know this is not exactly helpful to Phil, but how hard can it be to sit in a chair and stare at a medal?

Before she can get away, Phil grabs her by the arm and begs her to stay. "Please don't go, Alexa. We need you. Really, we do. You're the only one who can help us."

chapter two

Phil can really turn on the phony sentiment when he wants to. It's a handy skill to have, when you think about it.

With a mixture of reluctance and self-importance, Alexa sits back in her chair and crosses her arms. "If I feel his eyes on me again, I'm leaving and I'm never coming back."

Promise? I feel like saying. Instead I run upstairs and grab a Coke from the fridge.

I sit down at the kitchen table and drink it. Outside the leaves on the trees in our backyard are changing from summer green to orange and red. Another of life's miracles is descending upon us.

Whoopee.

Mom and Dad are into nature. They went on another one of their Autumn Walks this morning. They asked Alexa and me if we wanted to join them. Mom had on her safari hat and hiking boots. Dad had his camera strapped around his neck and wore his photographer's vest. Every pouch was filled with lenses, rolls of film and books about birds they never find.

"I'd rather die," said Alexa, to their offer.

"I'd rather she did too," I threw in for good measure.

They left without us.

I'm just about to look for something to eat when Phil comes running upstairs and asks me what I want Alexa to do.

This is not a question I'm used to answering. "Come again?"

"She's locked in," he says, his eyes wide. "She's hypnotized. I did it. She's down there with this totally serene look on her face. It's unbelievable."

I'm not hungry anymore.

I bolt downstairs. I have never seen my sister look serene before.

I stop in my tracks when I see her. She's sitting on a chair in the middle of our basement. Her back is straight. Her eyes are closed. Her face is passive, relaxed, devoid of all emotion—meaning, in her case, devoid of anger.

I see nothing evil about her for the first time in my entire life.

I kneel beside her. I want to test her to make sure this is real.

"Alexa?" Nothing. "Hey, wanna pizza? I'm buying." She doesn't move. "I saw your ex-boyfriend at the movies the other night. He was with his new girlfriend. They made out for two hours. Her bra was sticking out of his pants when they left." She remains limp.

I stand up and step back. "Wow."

Phil nods and continues to stare at his handiwork in amazement.

"Can we just leave her like this?" I ask him.

"Of course not."

"How come?"

He ignores me and picks up one of his books. "Her command word is Ophelia, from *Hamlet*," he whispers. "She told me that's the book she's reading. That's the word I used to get her into this trance. We'll use it to tell her what we want her to do. To snap her out of it, I say Cleopatra."

I nod. "Cool." It's more than that, I know, but I'm a bit stunned. I did not believe for one second that Phil could actually hypnotize someone. Alexa does have a small brain, though. This pretty much proves it.

"So, what do we do now?" I would like to just leave her like this. I could throw a blanket over her head and pull her over to the corner behind the pool table. I'd tell Mom and Dad she's at a friend's doing homework. What a fine day we could all have!

"Let's test her out," says Phil.

"How do you mean?"

"Let's give her something to do."

"Like what?"

Phil smiles. "I don't know, but whatever it is, it's gonna be fun."

chapter three

My name is Rufus Crowden, by the way. I'm in grade eight at Callton High in Callton, Alberta, north of Edmonton. It's a great place to live, especially if you have no need for lakes, rivers, shopping malls, theme parks, swimming pools, arcades, skateboard parks, movie theaters, McDonald's, Blockbuster—you get the picture. The population is about six thousand, but I have no idea why.

The first thing we do after Alexa is hypnotized is brainstorm a list of all the things we could get her to do.

"Why don't we print a big sign that says *Honk If You're Horny* and get her to carry it down the middle of Main Street?" I say, to get the ball rolling.

Phil looks at me and shakes his head.

"What's wrong with that? She won't know what she's doing."

He holds up his hand and counts his reasons. "One, she might cause an accident. Two, the cops will arrest her if they see her. Three, your mom and dad are out on a walk that may lead them back through town. Four, if any of these things happen, we'll be caught, killed and quartered by the time school starts in the morning."

"Which means no homework tonight," I say, to counter his attack. "So that's one for the 'Yes' side."

"Forget it," says Phil. "Think of something else."

"What about sending her over to do a singing telegram at old man Gleason's house across the street? We could dress her up like a showgirl from those musicals she watches all the time." Alexa's big into acting. Her closet is full of costumes and wigs.

"What if he dies?" says Phil.

"From what? She's not that bad. You've heard her sing before."

"I mean from excitement," says Phil. "Isn't that guy, like, ninety years old? What if he has a heart attack or chokes on his dentures?"

"Good point," I say sadly, although I really can't believe it would actually happen.

It's probably not something we should gamble with, though. Unfortunately.

"I have one," says Phil, finally. "Why don't we get her to make a bunch of phone calls to people. She can pretend she's the manager of an adult-only movie store and tell them that their X-rated movies are overdue."

"Now you're talking," I say. "She could call Mr. Ainsworth, our principal, and leave a message with his wife. She could say he has twenty movies out that were due a month ago. If he doesn't pay by tomorrow they're going to put his name on a sign outside the store."

"We could make up our own titles," says Phil, his eyes growing wide.

"Or, we could tell her that he's the grand prize winner of a contest he entered. We could make up our own prizes," I say. "Like a section of the store named in his honor."

Phil beams. "A weekend for two at Swingers Nightclub."

"A leading role in one of their movies."

"Let's do it," says Phil.

I stand up to get our phone from the kitchen, but then I remember something and sit down again. "We can't do it," I say.

"Why not?" says Phil. "It's perfect. No one will see us. We won't get caught."

"We only have one phone. Mom took the other one in last week to get it fixed. We won't be able to hear the people on the other end of the line."

"We can sit right next to Alexa," says Phil. "We can share the phone."

I shake my head. "That would never work. They'd hear us breathing and laughing. Besides, everybody has call display now. Ainsworth would be on our doorstep in two seconds."

Phil crosses his arms and pouts. "That was the best plan yet," he says.

"So think of a better one. Just don't include a phone."

A few minutes later, we hit on the plan we're going to use.

We decide to go easy on Alexa and give her a very simple set of instructions to follow. She's to be nice to Phil, Mom and Dad. I will be the foil. She is to treat me as she always does so no one, namely my parents, gets suspicious.

Phil explains this to her as she sits peacefully in her chair. Her head droops so her chin is almost touching her chest.

"Do you understand these instructions?"

Alexa nods.

Phil looks at me and crosses his fingers. "Okay, Alexa. Let's begin. When I snap my fingers, you will awaken and follow the directions I have laid out for you. You will not be aware that you are hypnotized, but you will recall the nature of the favor we asked of you. Are you ready?"

She nods once. "One. Two. Three." He snaps his fingers.

chapter four

Alexa raises her head, takes a moment to collect herself, looks at me and instantly scowls. "I told you I don't want you staring at me anymore." She rises to leave again. "Sorry, Phil. Get rid of your friend here and I'll help you out any way I can. Really. I mean it. I love your shirt, by the way. You look hot in it."

Phil's eyes nearly pop out of his head. Mine too, probably.

"Call me sometime." She moves toward the stairs. "When he's not around."

I don't want her to leave. This is way too good to end so quickly. "Please stay, Alexa. I won't stare at you anymore. I promise. I'll put a blindfold over my eyes."

She stops and turns around. "No." She starts to walk upstairs. Phil's shoulders sag. She looks at him and takes pity. "Aw, Phil. You know what? It's almost lunchtime. Can I fix you something to eat? A sandwich? Soup? A can of spaghetti?"

Phil brightens immediately. "I'd love some pancakes," he says. His favorite food in the world is pancakes. He can eat them anytime, day or night.

I brace myself. The last time I asked Alexa for anything she threw it at my head. I think it was a glass of water.

"What a great idea," she says, her face glowing. "I love pancakes. I'll make a batch right now. Do you like blueberry or raspberry?"

"Plain," says Phil. "Plain Jane."

"Plain Jane it is," says Alexa. "I'm right on it."

"I'm hungry too," I call out as she walks up the stairs.

"There's dog food in the cupboard. Help yourself."

Phil and I are thrilled. We high-five. We hug and dance in circles. Phil flops on his back on the couch and kicks his legs in the air like a dog scratching its back.

"This is so cool," he keeps saying.

Twenty minutes later, the door at the top of the stairs opens. "Phil, we're out of syrup. I can run to the store if you like. Or we can use brown sugar."

Phil settles himself before answering. "I prefer syrup, actually, if it's not too much trouble."

"Of course it's not. It's no trouble at all. I'll be back in twenty minutes. The table's all set, by the way. We can eat as soon as I get back."

Mom and Dad beat her home. My heart rate shoots up to about two thousand beats per minute when I hear them at the back door.

Phil tries to calm me down. "Everything's cool, remember? She's going to be nice to them too. We've accounted for this."

I need more assurance than that. "Phil, they're gonna know that something's up in two seconds. Alexa is never nice to them."

Check that. Mom and Dad take us on a warm-weather holiday every winter. They call it our family's migration vacation. Last year we went to Mexico for two weeks over Christmas. The year before we went to Hawaii. The year before that—Cuba.

Alexa is always very nice to them then.

Phil puts his hands on my shoulders and looks into my eyes. "Rufus, your sister has just cooked a batch of pancakes. She's not building bombs in the garage. She's not selling drugs out her bedroom window."

"That's not the point."

"No, Rufus, it is the point. She's not doing anything self-destructive. We're just having a little fun. No one's gonna find out about it."

"She's hypnotized, Phil."

"I know that. That was the purpose of all this, remember?"

We go upstairs.

The kitchen table is set for four. There is a small plate on the floor with a knife and fork beside it. I assume this is for me.

"What on earth is all this about?" Mom is standing in the kitchen. She has taken her boots off, but her safari hat is still firmly planted on her head.

"Alexa made pancakes." I try to sound as matter-of-fact as I can, but it's a challenge. I'd have better luck saying, "Hey, look. The leaves are turning back to green again. How cool is that?"

Mom and Dad look at each other.

"She did what?" says Mom.

"She made pancakes." Phil smiles proudly, as if Alexa was his little girl and she'd just set the table for a tea party.

"What's wrong with her?" Dad frowns. He's in the insurance business. When he isn't snapping photographs of ducks on a lake, or boring little birds in trees, he's telling people how much money they have to start socking away to pay for a decent funeral.

In other words, he can be a real bottom-line guy when he wants to be.

"I don't know," I say. "She's your daughter."

"I mean what's wrong with her right now? This morning."

I shrug and keep my lips sealed. The less said about this morning, the better.

Dad starts to think about it. I can practically see the gears and sprockets in his brain start to creak and turn.

"It's very nice." Mom finally takes off her hat. "I just don't think we've ever come home from a walk to anything like this before."

"It is pretty nice, isn't it?" says Phil, nodding in agreement and still looking extremely proud.

The four of us proceed to stand there and stare at the table that Alexa has prepared. It's like none of us know what to do, and we're all too stunned to even try and figure it out.

"Well then," says Dad, breaking the awkward silence, and apparently setting aside his concerns.

"Yes," says Mom, smiling and looking worried at the same time.

"I think I'll go wash my hands," says Dad. He leaves the kitchen. Mom runs after him like it's their honeymoon.

Phil and I just look at each other, grin like fools and shake our heads. Then the back door opens again.

Alexa bounds into the kitchen, shoves a bag of groceries into my face and says hi to Phil. "I bought some fresh fruit. Hope you like strawberries. Mom and Dad home yet?"

"They're getting washed." I put the bag down on the counter.

"I was asking him." Alexa points to Phil. He blushes a little. He seems to be enjoying the attention.

Mom and Dad return to the kitchen.

Alexa rushes toward them like they've just stepped off a plane from Afghanistan. "Mommy! Daddy! My God, it's so good to see you! Did you get any good pictures, Daddy? I know you were talking about needing a new wide-angle lens the other day. I wonder if this was a day you could have used it."

Dad's suspicions return. Big-time. His eyes dart around in search of clues to her high spirits—a letter from a friend in Winnipeg; her ex-boyfriend kneeling on the floor, begging for forgiveness; an empty case of beer.

Seeing nothing, he looks at me again, sees that I've been watching him and narrows his eyes.

chapter five

I try not to gulp, but I'm afraid I do anyway. I try not to rub my suddenly sweaty palms or rock back and forth on my feet, but I do anyway.

In the back of my mind, I hear myself trying to reason with him. "It's nothing bad, Dad. She's just hypnotized. Phil can snap her out of it in a second. I was hoping we could wait until she's done the vacuuming, though, and all my homework." I stop before reaching the part about getting the PIN number to her bank card.

It's funny how some ideas seem so terrific until you have to explain them to your parents.

Dad's mouth opens. He is just about to speak when...

"You know, Daddy, I've been thinking." Alexa unintentionally comes to my rescue. "I know there have been lots of changes at your work lately, and I heard you say to Mom the other day that you think there's going to be layoffs soon. So I was wondering, would this be a good year to skip the family holiday?"

The look on his face changes before my eyes from "What the devil is going on here?" to "Don't tell me what it is, just keep it going."

He looks at Mom, who appears ready to laugh, cry, shout, sing, ask questions and bury her head in the sand all at the same time.

In short, she is as confused as he is, but it's confused in a good way, so it doesn't matter as much.

"Daddy?" We all forget that Alexa is waiting for a reply to her question.

"Are you crazy, Alexa?" I say, before Dad can say anything. "We're not going to cancel our holiday. It's the only time of year we get along."

She turns and looks at me. "Don't be a drip, Rufus."

"Who's being a drip? Those holidays are a blast. We can't cancel."

"Think of someone else for a change, like your parents."

I can't believe I'm arguing with my hypnotized sister, but I am. "They like it too. Dad goes swimming with that dumb snorkeling kit of his. Mom gets a tan on the beach reading her books. They have a great time."

"Uh-huh, and who pays for it?" says Alexa.

"They do."

"Exactly."

"They're parents," I say to her, getting way more excited than I probably should. "They're supposed to pay for holidays. It's part of the job."

Alexa stares at me like I just stuck a fork in my ear. "You are so clued out it's frightening." Then she turns to Mom and Dad. "Daddy, Mommy, ignore him. I'm serious. If Daddy thinks we should stay close to home this winter, then that's where we should be."

It's not until I hear her say, "I'm serious" that I realize our family getaway is doomed.

Frantically, I look at Phil. Do something! I try to make my eyes say. He doesn't get the message. He's too busy smiling at Alexa.

It's up to me to think of a way out of this, but wait.

Did I just say that Phil was too busy smiling at Alexa?

I look at him again.

He is indeed watching and smiling at her, like a proud parent watching a child hand out cookies in a seniors' home.

No, it's different than that.

"Alexa, that is very thoughtful of you." Dad still looks like he thinks he may be dreaming.

"It certainly is." The same goes for Mom.

Alexa puts more pancakes on their plates. "Well, I just don't think we should have to fly halfway around the world just so we can be together without fighting. There's board games downstairs we can play. We could go tobogganing. Skating. Have a cookie-baking contest. Spend a fun day at West Edmonton Mall. I'd love to go to a movie with you guys. We haven't done that forever."

Again, Mom and Dad exchange looks. This time, I get in on it. I make eye contact with Mom, raise one eyebrow, make the cuckoo sign by my ear and motion toward Alexa.

Mom raises an eyebrow in response and takes a sip of her orange juice.

It's a very fine line I'm walking here. I'm trying to act as weirded-out by Alexa's bizarre change in attitude as they are, without giving anything away. I'm also fighting to keep our holiday alive.

"For what it's worth, I'd like it if you stayed." Phil finally opens his mouth. It's not exactly what I was hoping he'd say, but he's not saying it to all of us. He's speaking directly to Alexa. "I'll have nowhere else to go if you guys take off."

Phil is an only child. His parents both work twenty-six-eight, as in, twenty-six hours a day, eight days a week.

I know that's impossible. It's a joke he made up, his point being that he never sees them, and when he does, they're both too tired to do anything except watch TV and order pizza.

Alexa puts down her pancake flipper. She turns away from the stove and tips her head to one side, like she's talking to a dog. "Oh, Phillip. You are such a sweet boy."

Phillip? He's a prince in her eyes now?

Phil blushes. He shrugs and looks at his feet. "It's true," he says. "What else am I going to do? Besides..." He raises his eyes to Alexa's, and licks his lips, like he's about to say something really important. "I like coming over here."

Omigod. I'm not liking what I'm seeing here.

"Especially when you're here."

He's falling in love with her. That's what

that look was about. When she was telling Mom and Dad to cancel the expensive holiday, he wasn't staring at her like a father watching his daughter with a cookie tray. Phil was a lovesick fiancé watching the woman he loves teach African orphans the alphabet.

"It's only two weeks, Phil," says Mom, who has no idea how much I love her for saying that. "But that is if we go at all. Alexa, you raise a very good point about whether we should take a trip this winter. It may be that we decide to put it off for a year."

I take it back. As of this moment, I do not love my mother.

Alexa glows as she plunks another strawberry into her mouth. "Well, I say we settle it right now then. No holiday this winter, but plenty of family fun right here at home. And Phil, you're invited to spend every minute of it with us."

Phil beams back at her.

Mom and Dad, now looking like they've just won the lottery without realizing they had a ticket, dig into their pancakes.

Me? I say nothing. I do nothing.

What is there to say or do, other than to wish we had left Alexa alone with her stupid toenail clippers?

chapter six

Phil and I are not alone again until we're standing at the end of my driveway waiting for Alexa. The three of us are going for a walk together.

It was Alexa's idea, sort of—she asked Phil if he wanted to go for a walk with her.

He blushed, had trouble breathing, experienced at least one hot flash that coated his forehead in sweat and accepted.

I wasn't included, but I'm going anyway. I'm the tagalong. The third wheel. The guy in the backseat who won't shut up. The kid who won't go to sleep so his babysitter can sneak in her boyfriend.

I'm not proud to be going this way, but I'm not about to stay home and risk missing anything.

I've just accused Phil of having a crush on my sister.

He's looking at me like I said that the neighbor's tree just blew me a kiss.

"I beg your pardon?" he says.

I repeat myself.

"You think I have a crush on your sister?" he asks.

"Uh-huh."

He stares at me. He's trying to buy time. "Your sister, Alexa?"

"She's the only sister I have, Phil. I'm pretty sure you know that."

"For real?"

"Of course for real," I say. "Why would I make it up?"

He blinks and shakes his head. Then he does it again, this time adding a few smacks to the side of his head, as if there's some kind of internal malfunction in his brain that impedes his ability to decipher verbal messages. "Let me get this straight," he says, when he's finished.

"Please do."

"You think I have a crush on your sister, Alexa."

He's way overacting.

"Yes, I do."

"Prove it."

"I don't have to." I let him have it with a straight dose of silence. The proof has been right before my eyes all morning. His eyes too.

He blinks first. "That is the dumbest thing I've ever heard in my entire life."

I know that he knows I know.

"I've never heard anything so stupid... your sister...that's ridiculous. That is..."

Under my relentless glare, he starts to crumble.

"She's hypnotized, for God's sake. How could I fall for a person who doesn't even have her own mind?"

"That's precisely the reason." I break my silence and drive the dagger into his heart. "You've changed Alexa into your own personal robot. She's your Frankenstein, without the lug nuts on the side of her head. And she's not green."

His shoulders sag. His face contorts as the painful truth fights to break free.

Finally, like a person accused of committing a crime while sleepwalking, he confesses. "I don't know what happened." He shakes his head again.

I nod sympathetically. I'm the good cop now. The one he can talk to.

He opens up. "It started when she told me to give her a call. Then she offered me something to drink."

"She called you hot. That must have lit your fire."

"I could feel myself shaking as soon as she said it."

"You've never been called that before, have you?" Sometimes I know Phil better than he knows himself.

"I have so." He gives me an indignant look.

"Come on, Phil."

"Melanie Davis called me hot last year."
He says this as if he's speaking the truth.

"No, she didn't."

"She did so," he says again.

"Melanie Davis? Get a grip."

"In the weight room at school. She was looking for somebody and saw me and said, 'Hey, pretty hot there, Phil.' I swear to God. I was doing arm curls for phys ed."

I know Melanie Davis. She's tall. Blond. Wears more makeup than a drag queen. Has a boyfriend who is a drag queen. I know that doesn't make sense. I just don't like the guy. "I think she was being sarcastic," I say.

"No way. She said it right to my face." Phil looks so sincere as he talks.

"Really?" I ask.

"Absolutely."

I could pursue this further. I could ask if she laughed after she said it, or pretended to stick a finger down her throat. I could see if she's called him hot since then, or, if she's been hanging around the weight room, waiting for him to show up again. But I don't. I let it ride. Let him enjoy his little fantasy. "Well, okay then," I say to him. "I apologize."

"Thank you. I accept."

We're getting offtrack anyway. "But what are you going to do about Alexa?"

He takes a deep breath and lets it out slowly. Clearly he prefers talking about Melanie.

"I'm not sure," says Phil.

"You know that as soon as the spell's off, she's going to look at you like you're a hair in her soup again," I tell him.

"I've thought about that."

"She's not likely to call you hot," I say.

He nods reluctantly. I can see this is hard for him.

"Unless," I say, "you believe that she thinks you actually are hot."

chapter seven

He stops nodding and looks at me. He was not expecting me to say this. To be honest, I hadn't been expecting to say it either. Although the thought had crossed my mind.

"You mean she may be expressing her true feelings about me?" Phil asks.

I shrug. "I don't know. Isn't that what hypnosis is about, getting people to express things that they can't say when they're normal?"

A small but glowing curiosity returns to Phil's eyes. "Is it?"

"Well, you've read the books, not me. But I think I've heard that before."

Phil snaps his fingers. "You know what? You're right. I have read that."

"Have you?" I ask.

"For sure. I remember that now. For sure that happens. No question about it. Absolutely."

I nod my head. "So maybe she really does think you're hot. She's just never been able to say it before." I really cannot believe I'm saying this, but it does make a little bit of sense, I think.

"And that's why Melanie Davis could say it. Because she has more confidence than your sister. She's not intimidated by me," says Phil.

"Uh." That's not what I was trying to say.

"Wow." Phil ignores my hesitation. His face is aglow with excitement. It's as radiant as Alexa's red lipstick when she's on the make for a new boyfriend. "This is unbelievable."

"It *is* unbelievable." I truly agree with him on this point.

"This is amazing," he says.

"It's also just a theory."

He settles down a bit. "How could we prove it?"

I shrug. "I don't know." I start to think. Phil starts to think too.

He snaps his fingers before I do. "I have it."

"What is it?"

He smiles. "It's perfect."

"Let's hear it."

His eyes widen with delight. "Oh, this is gonna rock!" He punches his fist in the air. "It's gonna prove everything!" He sounds like a deranged physicist.

"What is it?"

He looks at me and calms down. "I can't tell you."

"What?"

"It's a surprise. I can't tell you. But you'll know what it is, don't worry. You'll figure it out. You have to, actually. You're a big part of it."

This is not the answer I want to hear. "Tell me what your idea is, Phil."

"I can't," he says. "It might spoil it."

"Spoil what?" I ask.

"I can't say."

I grab the collar of his jacket with both hands. "Phil, tell me what it is or I'll get ugly. I swear."

Phil looks me in the eye. He's ready to spill. I know he is. Then he looks up. His face breaks into an enormous relieved grin. "Alexa!"

My chance to hear his plan evaporates into thin air.

"Phil!" Alexa is dressed in blue jeans, walking shoes, a white sweater and a peach-colored hat and matching scarf. They're all clothes that Mom bought her for Christmas last year.

Alexa's never worn them before because they aren't black.

Just before she reaches Phil, she bends down and picks up a stick that's lying on our front lawn. She waves it under my nose, and then she flings it across the street. "Here, Fido. Go fetch. Phil and I want to be alone for a while."

She hooks her arm in his and they proceed down the sidewalk.

I follow a safe distance behind. But first, I run across the street and retrieve the stick.

I'll need it to jab Phil if he forgets to tell me what his plan is.

Or, more importantly, if I don't like it.

chapter eight

We walk through Callton's version of downtown.

There's not much to it.

It's a single street lined on both sides with stores and businesses. There's a bank on one side and a bar at the end of the other. Across the street from the bar is this Chinese restaurant called The Elegant Dragon. I threw up there once, all over the buffet table. Mom was very apologetic to the owner. She said I had the stomach flu.

I think it had more to do with Alexa telling me that the spicy beef was really mouse meat dipped in soy sauce.

I swear I saw a whisker after she said it—that's when the trouble started.

We keep walking until we get to the splashy part of town that has the new civic building, the Callton recreation center, the library and a trendy little coffee shop called C-Town Café.

Alexa always goes to the C-Town Café with her friends after school.

We stop just before we get to the doors.

Phil turns to me and whispers, "I'm going to change her spell."

"What?" I say. I'm not sure if I heard him correctly.

"He just told you to go to hell," says Alexa.

I shake my head. We really should have followed through with that singing telegram idea. Old man Gleason would have toughed it out...even if it killed him.

Phil whispers to me again. "I'm going to say Ophelia to change her spell. Stand over there."

I move away a few feet. But before I do, I give him a dirty look. What's he doing, saying this right in front of her? She's not supposed to hear him say that.

"Phil, what are you saying to Rufus?" she says as if she was following a cue. "If you want him to leave just throw that stick he has in his hand."

"Ophelia," says Phil loudly.

Alexa's head immediately droops so her chin is almost touching her chest. He whispers into her ear for about a minute. When he's finished, he steps away from her and goes inside the coffee shop.

A few seconds later, Alexa perks up again, looks around until she sees me standing ten feet to her right and bursts into a smile. "Well, hello stranger." She walks over and flings her arms around me in a big, loving, totally freaky embrace. "It's so good to see you again."

I smile back, return her hug and say nothing.

"You look terrific, as usual," she says staring right at me.

I have no idea what's going on anymore.

I am suddenly someone she wants to be with, and, apparently, Phil is not with us anymore.

Alexa is now just standing here, smiling at me. It's my turn to talk. I gulp instead. I assume we're long lost friends, but how long? And how lost? Why is she calling me a stranger all of a sudden?

"How are Mom and Dad?" She cuts me off before I can take my thoughts any further, which, as it turns out, is a good thing.

"Mom and Dad?" I ask. That doesn't sound like something one friend says to another, unless there's a "your" in front of it.

"Yes, remember them? Dad retired five years ago? Now he runs around with his camera making a nuisance of himself."

I stare at her, stunned. Dad didn't retire five years ago.

"No? You don't remember your father? How about Mom? She retired from her job at the library but still spends all her time there as a volunteer? You don't remember her either? Wow. I'm the one who's been in New York the past ten years, acting up a storm on Broadway. I thought I would have forgotten these things. You've been right here the whole time."

I need a second to compute this information. But that's all I need.

I get it now. We're still brother and sister, but it's ten years into the future and she's just returned home from New York. That was Phil's gift to her: Alexa's been talking about becoming a stage actress since she was old enough to breathe.

What about me, though? What did he tell her I do?

chapter nine

"So, how are things at the Dragon?" Alexa is talking to me again.

"The Dragon?"

She gives me another strange look. "Where you work? The Elegant Dragon? I understand you're the hot new sushi chef in town."

A sushi chef at The Elegant Dragon? Raw mouse? This is what he told her I do?

"I was surprised to hear that, but..." She gives me a shrug. "Who knew you liked food preparation?"

I start to shake my head, and then I stop. Now is not a good time to tell her she has it wrong. "Well," I say, trying to step into my new identity, "I always liked cooking. You know. Stirring soup and buttering toast and all that. I just wasn't comfortable telling anyone in case they made fun of me."

Alexa gives me a sympathetic look. "Oh, Rufus. I'm so glad you finally stopped worrying about what other people say. You have so much potential."

I'm staring directly into her eyes. My sister has never said anything remotely personal or inspiring to me before.

I'm moved by it, in a weird sort of way, given that it's not really my sister saying it. Still, it looks like her and sounds like her... but the words coming out of her mouth are different.

"Only you can make the you that you want to be, you know," she adds.

I frown. That one she might have to repeat.

"I mean, who knows? My acting career is going to the moon. Maybe someday you'll start showing people your fabulous writing."

My fabulous writing? Where did that come from?

"But, anyway, I'm sorry things didn't work out between you and Melanie. She's really a beautiful girl, beneath all that makeup. If it means anything, I'm sure you're not the only guy she's dumped."

Melanie? Melanie Davis? Phil told Alexa that I had a thing going with Melanie Davis?

"It's too bad it had to be so public, though. Right in the middle of the cafeteria? Was there anyone in your school who was not there to see it?"

"Uh." I start to shake my head. Wow. Phil really stuck it to me, didn't he? Maybe I shouldn't have grabbed him by the jacket so hard.

"At least it was your favorite soup she poured over your head, right? Cream of mushroom. Were you able to salvage any of it?"

I wince. "Not really. It was pretty mushy. And there were no crackers in it."

She smiles sympathetically. "Thank goodness you still have your sense of humor. I'm really sorry about Phil too, by the way. My God. What a shock that must have been."

What, there's more? Something happened to Phil?

"Thanks," I say, accepting her acknowledgment, even though I have no clue what she's acknowledging.

Alexa sadly shakes her head. "He was so young."

I'm caught off guard again. "So young to what?"

"To die," she says, her eyes reflecting her sorrow. "He was so young to die, Rufus. Your best friend. I felt so horrible when I couldn't get back here for his funeral. Rehearsals were going so poorly, though. There was no way they'd let me go."

I nod and try to look understanding. The lame character Phil has created for me is now clear: I cook raw food for a living in the worst restaurant on the planet. I'm extremely single. My best friend is dead.

Thanks, Phil. I owe you one. Maybe next time you could throw in overpowering body odor. And it's all just to find out if Alexa likes him for real or not. A variation on the old I-wonder-what-she-would-say-at-my-funeral thing.

"The funny thing is, I never really understood what you saw in him. I didn't get it. He wasn't funny. He wasn't smart. I totally murdered him every time we played Monopoly."

I smile at her. I love it when someone else's plan falls to pieces.

She sees me smiling. "What's so funny? I'm sorry, that's just the way I remember him. I mean, sure, he was reasonably good looking. He was polite. He was punctual."

I start to laugh. "Punctual?"

Alexa giggles. "Now what's so funny about that?"

I laugh even harder. "We should put that on his gravestone—*Phil Benson: Never late. Never early. Always right on time!*"

"Well, what am I supposed to say?" says Alexa. "I can't think of anything else."

She's laughing as hard as I am.

Poor Phil. I really should be feeling bad for him right about now. Maybe if he hadn't made me out to be such a loser I'd be sending a little pity his way. But he did, so I'm not.

Alexa's not finished either. "I mean, okay. He was more than just punctual. I shouldn't have said that."

"What else was he?" I have to hear more of this. She can be very funny when she wants to be.

"Well, he always took his shoes off at the back door. I know Mom appreciated him for that."

I laugh even harder.

"He washed his hands before dinner."

I nearly fall over.

"He always used a Kleenex. I never saw him wipe his nose on his sleeve or anything like that, or even pick his nose for that matter."

I'm laughing so hard that I seriously lose my balance. I start to fall but I bump into somebody walking toward the coffee shop.

"Watch it, you little puke." The guy gives me a shove.

I stop laughing and look at him.

I freeze. It's Alexa's ex-boyfriend, Scott. He's with his new girlfriend.

chapter ten

Alexa looks at Scott too. She's not laughing anymore.

"Hey, Alexa." Scott looks more nervous than I thought he would. "I thought you only came here on weekdays. You know Mona, don't you? Mona, this is...my friend, Alexa. Alexa, Mona."

Alexa doesn't say anything. She looks confused all of a sudden. Then I remember that she's still hypnotized. She's in a world ten years down the road from now. She may not even recall who Scott and Mona are.

"Of course," she says, a smile suddenly bursting across her face. "We've met, haven't we, Mona?" They shake hands.

Mona smiles back. She has a pointy little nose and beady eyes. She looks like that mouse I ate at the Dragon. "I'm not sure if we have or not," she says. She even sounds like a mouse.

"I'm here from New York, visiting my brother," says Alexa, to my horror. "You remember Rufus, don't you, Scott?"

I was really hoping she wouldn't say anything like that.

It's too late to worry about it now, though.

Scott looks bewildered. "What?"

Alexa turns on a beaming smile. "I'm an actress on Broadway. Oh yes! You didn't know that? I went right after high school. I landed my first role the same day I found a place to live! We had a party that night, I tell you."

Scott's bewilderment turns to fear.

"You know, you two should really come down to visit me sometime. You like live theater, don't you, Mona? You look like a theater buff. My apartment's too tiny for you to stay in, but, you know...New York's a big city. There's lots to do. Lots to see. And it never sleeps. I mean, really. Never. That is one cliché that is absolutely, one hundred percent true."

In perfect unison, Scott and Mona begin to slowly move backward as Alexa prattles on about life in the Big Apple.

Then Scott cuts her off. "What are you on, Alexa?"

She looks at him in surprise. "I'm not on anything, Scott. Why do you ask? I'm high on life, if that's what you mean. I'm high on my life. What are you two up to? You look very happy together. You married yet? Any kids? Do you live here in town or did you move into the city? Hey, have you tried the sushi at The Elegant Dragon lately? You'll never guess who's making it—my very own brother here—Rufus, sushi chef extraordinaire!"

Scott throws a nervous glance at me, and then he takes Mona by the arm and quickly guides her away from us. He's staring at Alexa as if he honestly believes she's mentally ill.

Mona does not protest. She seems to be as eager to scram as Scott is.

"Hey, where are you going?" says Alexa. "I was just going to offer to buy you a coffee. Sure I'm a starving actress but I get paid in American dollars."

They ignore her and scurry off.

Alexa's shoulders slump in disappointment. "What do you know? I finally meet some old friends and they run from me like I have ants crawling out of my ears. I can't believe I actually went out with that creep. He's all hands, you know that? Grabbing me here. Grabbing me there. I know what Mona must like if they're still together."

I feel sad all of a sudden.

"They've aged well, though, don't you think?" says Alexa. "Scott looks just like he did in high school."

I don't know why I feel sad.

Actually, I do know.

I'm sad because Alexa's going to go to school tomorrow and everyone will be all over her about what just happened. Scott and Mona are probably on their cell phones already, talking so fast they have to repeat everything three times just so their stories will be understood.

The problem is Alexa won't have a clue what anyone's talking about.

The more sincerely confused she looks, the more they'll think she's certifiably loony.

Tomorrow will be the longest, most miserable day of her life. The days after it won't be much better.

Is there anything I can do to prevent any of this?

I don't know. But the real question is, why do I care?

chapter eleven

"Did she say anything about liking me? Anything at all? Hurry, before she comes out," Phil asks. He is standing in front of me in the line at C-Town. Alexa has gone to the bathroom.

"Well, she did say you were punctual," I say.

Phil does not take this like a man.

"And that she never saw you wipe your nose without a Kleenex."

He's crestfallen. "She didn't say anything else about me?" he asks.

"Nothing," I say to him, hoping he can hear the satisfaction in my voice.

"Really?" He's crushed. He really is.

"Really."

"Did you ask her?" he persists. "Like directly?"

"After she explained to me that you were dead, yes, I asked her what she thought of you."

"And what did she say?" he asks again.

"I just told you," I say.

"That's it? That's all? Nothing about the good times we had?"

I frown. "What good times?"

"The pancakes. Spending Christmas holidays together. All that stuff."

"Phil," I say, "you just ate the pancakes. We haven't spent Christmas together yet. And there is no other stuff. You are not lifelong friends with Alexa. Face it. You're not even day-long friends with Alexa. You're an afternoon-long friend, and even that's about to end."

He's demoralized. Again I feel an urge to cushion his disappointment. I am grateful when the urge passes. But I do explain my position. "Maybe if you hadn't made me out to be such a putz, I would have sold you to her a bit better. Talked you up a bit more. You know what I'm saying?"

It doesn't matter if he does. As soon as Alexa comes out of the bathroom, he has to make like a stranger in front of me in line, so this conversation can't last forever.

His sadness turns into confusion.

I pay no attention. "I mean, really. A sushi chef at The Elegant Dragon? That's what you see me doing ten years from now? What, all the paper routes in town already taken? No shopping carts at the grocery store to collect?"

He gives me a funny look. "What are you talking about?"

I look to the bathrooms before answering. Alexa's coming out. "Turn around," I hiss at him.

Phil whirls around so Alexa doesn't see him.

I'm not sure what he's thinking, but if it's something like, The next time we do this, I'll make Rufus a bit more successful, then it's all been worthwhile.

"You don't have to work today, do you?" Alexa's joins me just as Phil steps forward to place his order. The back of his shoulders stiffen as he hears her voice. It must be agony to find out that the one you loved barely knew you were alive. Or maybe he's bummed out because he realizes that his plan wasn't so golden after all.

"No, it's my day off," I say to her. "Too much time in the kitchen and I lose my touch."

"Must be nice. When I'm in a play, it's day after day after day of rehearsals, costumes, makeup, performances. Sometimes I sit backstage thinking about how nice it would be to actually have time to see a play on Broadway," she says.

"It must be heaven for you," I say.

She looks at me and smiles. Check that. She glows. "Oh, Rufus, I just love it out there. I have so many friends and they all accept me for who I am and I accept them for who they are. It's like Winnipeg all over again, only bigger. And I get paid for it."

As she says this, I'm reminded of how difficult the move to Callton was for her. She had a ton of friends in Winnipeg. She was a member of one of the top drama groups in the province. She had a boyfriend who wasn't a jerk.

We moved to Callton because Dad got transferred. Alexa cried in the car for nine hundred miles while I sat beside her and stared out the window.

I wasn't exactly thrilled with the deal myself. I had friends in Winnipeg. I had my place at school and in the community. I was in the mix there, if you know what I mean. I was comfortable. I knew my way around.

In Callton, I don't know anything.

I've been here for a year now and I still feel like I don't belong. I have exactly one friend—Phil—and that's it.

I buy Alexa a large latte and a low fat, mixed fruit, bran muffin. It's her choice. She balks when I tell her that I'm buying, but when I tell her it's probably the only time

I've ever bought her anything in her life, she gives in with a laugh. "Don't exaggerate so much. You're a great little brother."

She stops at the condiments stand on her way to our table and nearly bumps into Phil, who may as well be baking a cake for all the time he's taking.

"Oops, I'm sorry." Alexa narrowly avoids spilling her latte.

"No problem." Phil stands there staring at her. He looks so heartbroken. He looks like he's about to break into a country song.

"Are you almost done there?" Alexa asks him. "I just have to grab a napkin."

He steps out of her way.

She takes a napkin and walks over to join me at our table. "Did you see that guy I just about bumped into? Doesn't he look like somebody you know? Or used to know?"

I pretend to look around the coffee shop. "Who? What guy? I wasn't watching."

"That tall guy sitting by himself near the washrooms. Don't look. He's staring right at us."

I look anyway and wave.

"Rufus, stop it. You're going to get us into trouble."

Poor Phil. He looks like he just swallowed a plate of my sushi.

"What. It's some guy staring at you," I say to her. "Maybe he recognizes you from a play."

"Yeah, right. Except no one around here ever goes to plays."

"Maybe he's a movie director looking for the next big star," I say.

Alexa snorts into her latte.

"Why not?" I ask.

She drops her voice and pretends she's a man. "Boss, I'm going to find the next starlet. Marilyn Monroe, Nicole Kidman and Lindsay Lohan all rolled into one. I'm starting up in Canada. In a remote dust bowl, a prairie town called Callton. I'll phone as soon as I find her."

I laugh again. Alexa can do impersonations of men better than most men can.

I watch her as she takes a sip of her drink and looks toward Phil. "Uh-oh. He's coming over here."

chapter twelve

By the time I turn my head Phil is standing next to our table. Before I can say anything, he says "Ophelia" to Alexa.

Immediately her eyes close and her head slumps forward so her chin taps against her chest. Thank God he gave her a chance to put her drink back down on the table. She'd be wearing it right now if he hadn't.

Phil pulls up a chair and sits down.

"Tired of being dead, I take it?" I say to him.

He scoffs. He's still looks sad, but he also looks angry. "Tired of being laughed at is more like it. Tired of being the butt of all your jokes."

"We weren't laughing at you," I say unconvincingly.

"Of course you were."

"All right, so what? It was your grand idea."

"My idea was completely different than this," he says, shaking his head.

"You just wanted to hear Alexa say you were hot again."

Phil frowns and looks at me as if that's the most bizarre thing he's ever heard in his life, which it is, when you think about it.

"Come on," I say, because I know I'm right. "Admit it. That's what this was all about."

In spite of himself, he starts to smile.

"Come on, boy. You can do it. Come on," I encourage.

He starts to blush.

"Take it one word at a time. Yes. Rufus. I. Want. To. Hear. Her. Say."

"All right. Cut it out." He waves me off. "So what? Who cares what I wanted her to say? It was a bad idea. I can see that now. I'm sorry I did it."

"You mean dying at such a tender young age or hypnotizing Alexa in the first place?"

"Dying at such a tender young age," he responds.

I take a sip of my drink. "Good. Because I have a favor to ask you."

"What is it?"

"I want you to try and hypnotize me again." I say this with a straight face because I am serious.

"What?" he says.

"I want you to try and hypnotize me again. I have some things I want to say to Alexa."

"Are you serious?" he asks.

"Absolutely."

"What kind of things?"

"Personal things," I tell him. "Between me and her."

He leans forward in his chair, like Oprah does when her guests are about to say something that may actually be interesting. "Like what?"

I lean toward him. "Didn't I just say they were personal?"

"Yeah? So? Didn't I just admit that I wanted her to say I was hot again?"

"No."

"Well, I am now," he says. "That was the reason I died. I wanted to hear her say it. I wanted to hear her say she was crazy about me and that her greatest regret was that she didn't say so while I was alive. So come on. Now you have to tell me. What kind of things do you want to say to her?"

I take a minute to level with him. "Phil, do you know what the word 'personal' means?"

"Yes."

"Good," I continue. "Then don't take this personally. I have some things I want to say to my sister that are between me and her. Period."

He sits back in his chair and frowns at me. "Is that why you wanted me to hypnotize you in the first place?"

"What?" Where did that question come from?

"Is that why you were so gung ho about being hypnotized, so you could say something nice to Alexa?"

"No." Phil seems to be in need of a quick history lesson. "I said yes to being hypnotized because you asked me if I wanted to be hypnotized. You needed someone to practice on, and I thought it sounded cool."

This is all true, but it's not the complete truth.

I haven't been the happiest camper in the village lately. This school counselor I've been seeing, Mrs. Roland, thinks I may be depressed. One of my teachers sent me to see her because he said I look too glum all the time.

Mrs. Roland asked me last week if there were any troubles at home that I wished to talk about. I told her about the constant state of conflict I was in with Alexa. She asked me if I liked that, and I said no. Then she asked me what my preferred relationship with Alexa would be. I said that I wish we could be friends, since I have only one other friend at the moment.

"Why can't you say something personal to her when you're normal?" says Phil.

I look at him like he's crazy. "Can you imagine me sitting down with Alexa and asking her if she would like to be my buddy?"

Phil shrugs. "Why not?"

"Why not?" I ask him. "Why not? Why not?"

Phil looks around before answering. I think he's concerned we may be drawing attention to ourselves. I am starting to get a bit worked up here. Who knows? Maybe I am depressed.

He leans forward and whispers, "Yeah. Why not?"

I continue to stare at him, but say nothing. It is actually a pretty good question. I've thought of writing something to her before. As Alexa mentioned earlier, I like to write. Nobody knows this about me but Mom, Dad and her. Alexa found out entirely by accident: Mom left a poem I wrote on the kitchen table one morning and Alexa saw it, read it and didn't say anything about it. She either liked it or didn't get it. At least she didn't hate it, or worse, make fun of it.

One of the reasons I like writing is because I can say things that I would never be able to say out loud, especially to someone like my sister. It's a step removed from an actual face-to-face interaction.

So why don't I just do it then—write something and leave it on her desk or send it to her as an e-mail? It's still too close, that's why. Besides, if she didn't like what I said, or thought it was stupid, I'd be dead. She'd have my words posted on the Net in thirty seconds.

"Good question," I say, after taking a deep breath. "I don't know why. I'll have to think about that."

"Okay," says Phil, obviously relieved that I've settled down. "While you're thinking about that, can you also think about what I do with her if I hypnotize you?"

He motions toward Alexa, who's curled peacefully in her chair like a cat taking a nap.

"What do you mean?" I ask. "Just bring her back to normal. You guys can have your fun, and then I can say what I want to say to her."

"She'll be nasty again. She won't want anything to do with us."

I disagree. "Sure she will. I'll be completely in her hands. It'll be a dream come true for her."

"Okay." Phil sits back in his chair. I can tell he's considering my request. "How do you know what you're going to say?"

"Just command me to be nice to her. The rest will take care of itself."

"How do you know?"

"Because Alexa said some things to me that made me feel good. I'm sure I'm capable of doing the same."

He's still skeptical. "And if you don't?"

"How can my relationship with her get any worse?" I say. "When she's not hypnotized we hate each other."

"My relationship with her sure got worse."

"Well," I say with a shrug, "you were stupid."

"Thank you."

"You're welcome," I say. "Now get your medal out."

chapter thirteen

After twenty minutes of intense concentration and complete failure, Phil finally admits that he's forgotten how to hypnotize people.

"You've what?" I say.

He looks totally confused, like a guy who can't find his keys, or his car, or even the parking lot he left it in. "I can't remember how to do this. I must be missing a step."

"Are you sure you forgot?" I say.

"Of course I forgot. Look at her." Phil motions toward Alexa, who's head has just lulled from one shoulder to the other. "Exhibit A."

"I *am* looking at her. I'm looking at her and saying to myself, 'Is there such a thing as beginners' luck when it comes to hypnosis?' because I don't know how else to explain this."

Phil scoffs at the idea. "Of course not."

"Well, why can't you do it again?"

"I just told you why. My books are in your basement. I have no resources here," he says.

"You have your medal," I remind him.

"That's not enough."

"You have your brain. I thought you said you've been studying this stuff for years?"

He shakes his head. "No, I said I read my first book about hypnosis three years ago."

"What's the difference?"

"I haven't been reading about it constantly since then. I read a book three years ago. Six months later I read another book. A year later I read another book." He shrugs as if to underline the randomness of his study habits.

I shake my head. The guy who once hailed himself as a scholar on the subject is quickly becoming the Accidental Hypnotist. "What about the course you took?" I ask.

"What about it?" he asks.

"Do you not remember anything from it?"

He hesitates before answering. "No."

"Well, what kind of a course is it if a week after you take it you can't remember anything?" I say.

Phil looks down at the table. He seems uncomfortable. When he looks up again, he's blushing. He looks back down and takes in a deep breath. "I didn't actually take the course, all right?"

"Excuse me?"

He starts talking to the table again. "It was more expensive than I thought it would be. My dad said no when I asked him for the money. I didn't actually take the course."

"You didn't take it?" Now it's me who needs clarification.

"No, but I still learned quite a bit from it. I read the whole introduction. It talked about command words and all that. How the brain works."

"How the brain works?" I scoff. "You learned about how the brain works by reading the introduction of a course?"

"Part of the brain." He holds his thumb and forefinger a fraction of a millimeter apart. "You know. A bit. But it was more than I knew before. Believe me. I had to read it twice."

I sit back in my chair. I'm deflated. My shoulders sag. My big chance to say something meaningful to my sister and it's gone before it gets here.

Now I'm definitely depressed.

Phil carries on as if I just bought him a cookie and asked him to tell me more. "It was good, though, you know. I told my dad I didn't need his credit card anymore. He was happy about that."

I smile and raise my eyebrows. Good for you, Phil, I say to myself. Too bad you forgot it all.

"So, I guess I should say I'm sorry," he adds, a little too late. "I kind of oversold myself there."

I nod again and shrug. I really have no idea what I'm supposed to say here. My best friend's just come clean about lying to me about what we've been doing all day. In the meantime, my sister, who apparently has a brain the size of a pea, is patiently waiting for her next command.

"Are you mad at me?" he asks.

"A little." I could say a lot, but I'm not sure what good it would do.

"I didn't mean to mislead you, you know," he says.

"But you did. You made me think that you really knew what you were doing."

"Well," he pauses and points to Alexa, "obviously, I do know what I'm doing. I just...don't know how to do it again."

"No." I disagree with him. "You got lucky, Phil. This is not the result of someone who knows what he's doing."

We both look at Alexa.

"That's not true," he says.

"Sure it is," I say. "How else can you explain it? You've just told me you don't know half of what you said you knew. The other half you've forgotten. I'd have better luck being hypnotized by a dog right now."

"Get lost," he says, waving me away.

"It's true. You have no idea how you hypnotized Alexa. You couldn't do it again to save your life."

"I think that's an exaggeration."

"I don't think it's an exaggeration at all," I say. "It's probably an understatement."

"I never said I was an expert," says Phil, in a weak attempt to defend himself. "But you know what? I must know something about it because look—she's been doing everything we've asked all day. She's been nice to me. Nice to you. Nice to your mom and dad."

"Come on, Phil." I shake my head. All of a sudden, I want this day to be over. "This Ophelia crap, and whoever that other chick is, Cleo-whatever, it's all pure luck. We should have gotten Alexa to buy us a lottery ticket when she went out to get the pancake syrup."

"That's how you do it, Rufus. Those were her command words."

"Whatever."

"And that chick is Cleopatra."

I shrug. I could care less what her name is. And to be honest, I'm not even that mad at Phil about embellishing his credentials. I'm just disappointed that he's not able to hypnotize me.

None of that matters anymore, though.

At the mention of the word Cleopatra, Alexa immediately snaps out of the spell she's under. She's staring at us now with a peculiar, confused look on her face.

She's not serene anymore.

She's angry.

chapter fourteen

"What the hell am I doing here?"

Her eyes are darting between Phil and me. We're both very frightened. Her eyes are burning holes through our faces. Her nostrils are flared like a bull's. Her lips are turning white. Her fingers are curled into tight little fists.

Alexa is not above causing a scene in public, and if she manages to get the truth out of one of us, or figures out for herself that she was brought here in a trance, all bets are off on how she may react.

Will she call the police and cry that she's been kidnapped and removed from her house against her will?

Possibly.

Will she tell Mom and Dad?

Probably, unless we can bribe her to keep her mouth shut.

Will she hold this against me for the rest of my life?

Yes.

Will any or all of these scenarios mark the end of my life as I have known it for the first thirteen years?

Absolutely.

"Tell me you little pukes or I'll pour those scalding hot drinks down your pants."

Phil licks his lips and gulps. It looks like he has a golf ball lodged in his throat. His breathing is becoming shallow.

There is more at stake for him here than there is for me, since he was the one who actually did the hypnotizing. Although, as he just demonstrated, he'll never be able to prove it.

Nevertheless, if Alexa does call the police, and if charges are laid, they will lay them against both of us: hypnosis in the first degree against Phil, accomplice to the crime against me.

"Phil," says Alexa, directing her smoldering heat at our weakest link, "tell me what I'm doing here or I'm calling the police." She reaches into her hip pocket and removes her cell phone. She flips it open and turns it on.

Phil looks like he might die.

He's come a long way from happily eating her pancakes and encouraging her to stay home so they can hang out together over the holidays.

"I, I." He suddenly has a stutter. He licks his lips again. Drips of sweat slowly roll down his forehead to his cheeks. His hands begin to shake.

Disappointed or not, frustrated or not, upset or not, I must come to my friend's defense. I can no longer sit and watch him melt into his T-shirt and pants.

I have an idea.

"Hey, Alexa," I say, my voice light and happy, my eyes wide with pretend joy. "Phil told me you'd be here. Wow. Has it really been ten years? You look great!"

Alexa looks at me like I have snakes crawling out of my nose. "Are you sick?"

"Me? No, I'm fine. I'm fantastic, actually, now that I've got that book tour out of the way."

"That what?" she says, looking confused and repulsed at the same time.

"Oh, my publisher sent me on this crazy cross-country book tour thing. God. You haven't lived until you've read to a seniors' book club in a Des Moines, Iowa donut shop at nine o'clock in the morning."

It's working. I can see clearly that Alexa is not mad anymore. Is she thoroughly confused? You bet she is. But no sister ever called the cops because she couldn't understand what her brother was talking about. Or at least, no cop ever bothered to check it out.

"Still acting?" I continue. This is fun, when you get the hang of it. Alexa should try it in one of her drama classes sometime. "You know, you really should get in touch with that troupe you were with in Winnipeg. I bet they've taken a few of their shows on the road by now. They'd love to have you go with them. You'd take those shows to a whole new level."

She stares at me, and then she looks back at Phil, who, in turn, looks at her and then at me. By the time he looks back at Alexa, he knows what's going on.

He smiles at her. "Meet the new Rufus, Alexa. He's the nicest guy you'll ever meet in your life."

"Excuse me?" Alexa is slower to buy in.

"I've hypnotized him. He's ten years into the future. He's just come back for a visit."

"Get lost."

"I'm serious," he says. "He's hypnotized. Totally."

"How stupid do you think I am, Phil?" she says.

"You're not stupid at all. I swear to you. He's in a trance as we speak. He's hypnotized. Just like you were."

This gets her attention. "Are you serious?"

"Of course," he says, with a huge smile on his face. It's mostly a smile of relief, but she doesn't have to know that.

"I was actually hypnotized?" she says.

"Yes."

"And that's how I ended up here?" she asks.

"Exactly."

"Omigod." She covers her mouth with her hand. She is genuinely surprised.

"Watch this." He turns to face me. I look at him and smile. Apparently I've decided to be nice to both of them. "Rufus," he says, and then he hesitates. I believe it's time for him to say the command word he's given me, but of course, since he hasn't given me one, he has no clue what it is.

"Yes?"

We stare into each other's eyes. In any other context, this would be extremely uncomfortable. Given that we're attempting to save our lives, however, it's not so bad.

"Rufus, what year is it?" he says. Maybe he wasn't thinking of a command word.

"Why, it's 2017, Phil. Why do you ask?"

"No reason. Just curious." He turns back to Alexa, smiles and raises his eyebrows. "Pretty good, eh?"

"That's amazing," says Alexa. "That's awesome."

"Thank you," says Phil. He looks proud of himself again, as if he had actually hypnotized me.

"So we can do whatever we want with him?" says Alexa, with a small yet growing gleam in her eye.

"Uhh," says Phil. "Well..." He looks uncomfortable again.

So do I, I'm sure, but it beats having to apply skin moisturizer to my burnt privates, which is exactly what I'll be doing if Alexa discovers the truth.

"You can talk to him and everything," says Phil. "Find out where's he's at. That's what we did with you."

Alexa ignores him. The gleam in her eye has grown into a ray of pure delight. "Hey, Rufus," she says, staring intently at me. "Why don't you pop into the ladies' washroom over there and get me a Kleenex?"

I hesitate, but only for a moment. "Sure," I say. "I could use the exercise. Too much time sitting in airplanes these last few weeks."

"Attaboy," says Alexa, moving her feet so I can get by her. "You may as well go pee in there while you're at it. No point getting up twice."

I gulp, but she doesn't catch it. "You got that right," I say, before marching off.

"And sing! You have a beautiful voice, remember?"

I turn around to face her. For a brief moment, I'm about to tell her everything. Then I see Phil, whose eyes are begging me to do whatever she asks, which reminds me that I pretty well have to do whatever she asks. So I flash her a big thumbs-up and break into a sensational version of "My Humps" by the Black Eyed Peas.

I walk straight into the women's bathroom, shut the door and lock it. It's empty, thank God. Then a toilet flushes. I forgot to check the stall behind the door. I lunge for the door of the other stall, but before I can swing it open and hop inside to safety, I see the big bold sign in thick black marker that's taped to it: *Do Not Use! Out of Order! If you Flush It, You Clean It!*

I hear a familiar voice. "Rufus? Is that you?"

chapter fifteen

I whirl around. It's Mrs. Andreason, my science teacher. She lives here in Callton. I see her all the time at the grocery store or riding her bike with her husband.

"Mrs. Andreason, hi!" I say without having to fake in any way that I'm surprised to see her. "How are you?"

"I'm fine," she says, her face falling quickly into a frown. "Why are you in here?"

"The mens' bathroom is out of order," I say. "And I really have to go." I cup my hands in front of myself and squat a little, to show her I'm not lying, even though I am.

"No, it's not. Darren just used it."

"Did he?" I say, wishing something heavy would fall on my head.

"Yes, he just came out a minute ago."

"Did he break it? Because my friend Phil said I had to use the ladies' room."

Mrs. Andreason gives me that I'm-fed-up-with-your-antics look that all teachers have at their immediate disposal and rolls her eyes. "Phil?"

"Yeah. Phil Charles, from school," I say as if to suggest that my source is a reliable one.

"And you believed him?"

"He said he wasn't joking."

She shakes her head and moves by me. "I'm glad it's the weekend, Rufus. Otherwise you'd be down in the office by now. Don't pull this stupid stunt at school." She pulls on the door, but of course it's locked, so it doesn't open. She pulls on it again. Then she turns around.

"What's going on here, Rufus?"

I'm about to try and come up with an answer when someone on the other side of the door starts to bang on it and yells, "I can't hear you singing in there! Come on, Rufus! Belt it out!"

It's Alexa.

In a weird way, I'm glad it's her. I am probably very close to being in serious trouble here, standing next to my female science teacher in a locked women's bathroom.

Immediately, I start to sing again. "I met a girl down at the disco. She said hey, hey, hey, hey, let's go."

I reach past Mrs. Andreason, unlock the door and open it for her. She steps out.

Alexa is leaning against the wall, killing herself laughing.

Mrs. Andreason looks at her, then at me, and shakes her head. "Meet me at the main office tomorrow at nine o'clock, young man. We are not going to have this kind of conduct from our students in this town."

Then she leaves, thank God, or else I'd have had to tell her that I don't go to her school anymore, but that I'd be happy to return to give a free reading of my latest novel to her students.

"That was priceless," says Alexa between gasps for air.

"Here's your Kleenex," I say to her. She actually needs it now, to wipe the tears off her cheeks.

We return to our table, where Phil now looks like he's swallowed a few too many laxatives.

"Omigod, that was funny," says Alexa. "I love this. Thank you so much, Phil."

He looks at her but doesn't say anything. I think he feels badly about what I've just been through, but I can't tell for sure. He may just be feeling badly, period.

"I like you in that shirt, by the way," adds Alexa. "You look hot in it."

Phil's eyeballs nearly spring out of their sockets. In an instant, all that ailed him a split second ago is gone from his mind.

"You seeing anyone right now?" she asks him, a coy look in her eye.

He can't talk. I can see him trying, but absolutely nothing is coming out.

"Yes? No?" she prods, before turning to me. "How about you, lover boy? Was that your wife you were singing to in the toilet?"

I can't believe what's going on here. Did she just say to Phil what I thought she said?

"Hey, you. Stephen King, or whatever you call yourself. Are you married these days or what?"

"Me? No. I'm, I'm, I'm..." I realize that I've never talked about this to Alexa before. She's never asked about girls I may be interested in, and I've never offered to tell her.

"Gay?" she says, leaning toward me. Then she sits back. "Of course you are. I should have known. That's why you read those poetry books all the time."

I frown at her. "I don't read poetry. I read science fiction."

"Whatever."

"And I'm not gay."

"I know you're not, Rufus," she says, with a gentle smile. "I'm only joking."

I ignore her. "As a matter of fact, I'm seeing a very lovely playwright at the moment. She's from Paris."

Alexa's eyes grow wide. "Paris? Wow. Are you sure that's not her name?"

"I'm positive."

"Good for you." She continues to smile at me. "I'm happy for you. That's exciting. I knew you'd make it as a writer someday."

"Thank you." This is my big chance to say something sweet to her. "It's because of you, you know."

"I beg your pardon?" Now she looks confused.

"I said to myself, 'If she can be such a wonderful actress, why can't I be a writer?' You inspired me to be who I am today."

"Really?" she says.

"Really," I say.

"Wow. I never expected to hear you say that."

"It's true," I add. "What can I say?"

Alexa looks pleased. "So, what am I up to these days then?" she asks.

I lick my lips. I'm staring at her, but I can't speak. What else do I want to say to her? I don't know. At least, I don't think I know. It may have something to do with wanting to tell her that we're friends again, like when we were kids building play forts in the basement with every blanket in the house, or riding our bikes to the candy store across the street from Assiniboine Park in Winnipeg, or lying awake together on Christmas Eve because we were too excited to sleep.

"You're everything you always wanted to be," I blurt.

Her eyes go wide with surprise, and then they narrow into a frown. "What do you mean?"

"I mean, you're a star actress on Broadway, and you have the best sound system known to mankind in your apartment, and you have a boyfriend whose Turkish." These are all the things that Alexa constantly talks about, especially the Turkish boyfriend.

"How do you know this?" she says.

"Because I just got back from visiting you in New York. I saw your latest show. I slept on that crappy foldout couch you have in your one-room apartment near Central Park. And we had a fabulous dinner together. You, me and...Tamuk. He's your co-star in your latest play."

Alexa stares at me for several seconds. Her face is expressionless. She does not look shocked by what I've just told her, or surprised, or, for some weird reason, even particularly happy. Then, slowly, a small smile begins to creep across her face.

"It's true," I say to her. "Life is good all around. Even Phil here got a promotion. He's the new top dog at Farley's Pet Supplies over there in the Callton Industrial Park. Right, Phil? You were pretty excited about that when you called me last week." There, I say to myself. Now we're even.

Phil gives me a lame smile, but not too lame. He's still living off the thrill of hearing Alexa call him hot again, this time for real, apparently.

"Well, that is really quite amazing, Rufus," says Alexa. "I don't believe any of it, but that imagination of yours is remarkable. You really should spend more time writing."

Now it's my turn to frown. "What do you mean you don't believe any of it?"

She smiles sweetly at me. "I'm saying you can stop now," she says, her eyes locked on mine. "I know you're not really hypnotized. Thank you for indulging me by going into the ladies' bathroom, though. That was very brave of you. I'll be sure to send a note to your teacher when you meet her at the office tomorrow morning."

"What are you talking about?" I say to her. Now I'm worried again that she's going to raise hell about being brought here against her will.

"Let me put it in plain English for you," she says. "You're full of it. And he's full of it too. But don't worry. I'm not upset. You wanna know why? Because I'm full of it also."

chapter sixteen

It was all a hoax.

Right from the beginning.

There was not one microsecond when Alexa was anything but pretending to be hypnotized.

"Are you kidding me?" she says, looking at Phil. "Did you really think you could hypnotize me by waving that little medal in my face? Did you not think for one second that there may be more to it than that?"

I stare at Phil. "Is that all you did?"

"No," he says defensively. "I did more than that."

"You did not," says Alexa, laughing. "You had no clue what you were doing. Thank God, Rufus ran upstairs to the kitchen or I never would have been able to fake it."

I shake my head. Here I thought it was really just a matter of Alexa having a smaller brain than me. Now I find out Phil has the small brain. Or is it my brain that needs a steroid injection? Maybe it's both of us. We were both duped. We both thought Alexa was hypnotized. Neither one of us thought for a second that she may be pulling a fast one.

"Why did you fake it?" I say to her.

She looks at me and smiles. "Oh, lots of reasons really. I was bored. I had a drama assignment to do. My friend Tonya was staying at her dad's all weekend and wasn't going to get home until tonight."

"What was your drama assignment?" I ask.

"Get this," says Alexa. "It was, 'Get into a role-playing situation without telling anyone what you're doing, and see how long it takes them to figure it out.' Isn't that amazing? What a perfect exercise. And you two dolts never did clue in. My God, Rufus, I should have asked you to run naked around the outdoor track. You would have been out there in all God's glory until the cops showed up."

I look at Phil. "We should have gone with the 'Honk If You're Horny' idea. That would have put her on the spot."

Alexa laughs again. "That was such a good idea. I was so worried you were going to go with that one. I'm glad you chickened out, Phil. I have no idea what I would have done."

I glace over at Phil. He looks like I feel— crappy.

I want Alexa to leave so we can mope in silence.

I know this whole thing started as fun, but when she told me that she thought I was a fabulous writer and encouraged me to break out of my shell, I believed she meant it. Now I find out she was joking, collecting fodder to share with the rest of her drama class.

Or was she?

"You probably want to know a few things, right?" she prattles on, before I can interject. "Like, why did I try so hard to talk Mom and Dad out of our winter holiday? And what am I going to do when I see Scott at school tomorrow?

"Well, first, Dad was so on to you, Rufus. He was ready to eat you alive. Phil, you were dessert. He wasn't thinking hypnosis, but he sure knew something was up. I threw out that cancel-the-holiday idea because I'd heard them talking the night before about his problems at work. That was the only thing that would get them thinking about something other than what was going on with me.

"As for Scott? We got lucky with Scott. Mona's not really his girlfriend. He's two-timing on Jessica Perkins with her. I checked my cell phone in the bathroom. He's already left two messages begging me to pretend we didn't see each other. He said nothing about how weird I was acting."

"Well done," I say. It was a very impressive performance, when you think about it, not that I want to spend too much time doing that.

"Thank you," says Alexa. She finishes off her drink. "You too."

"Not really." I shrug. I'm ready to leave now. Phil is sitting beside me, quiet as a mute. Considering this was his baby, he must be even more disillusioned than I am.

I prepare to leave.

"I had a lot of fun with you guys today, you know," Alexa adds, before I can stand up. She raises her eyes so they're on mine. "I mean it. That was a riot."

Open communication does not come naturally in my house. We don't have family meetings. We have no pizza nights or once-a-month Sunday brunches in the city where we laugh and talk about whatever we feel like. We don't say good night to each other before bed. Half the time, we don't even say good-bye when one of us leaves the house. We used to. Just not anymore.

"It was fun, wasn't it?" I say, because it truly was.

"It reminded me of what a jerk you are sometimes," says Alexa.

"Excuse me?" I say. Aren't we entering a phase of the conversation where we're all nice to each other?

"You can be such a jerk sometimes. Today you were a jerk in the morning, but for the rest of the day you were a blast. The contrast is just...startling."

"Do you think that has anything to do with how you treat me?" I say.

Alexa thinks about that for a moment. "I don't want to fight all the time anymore," she says, finally. "I don't want to wake up angry and go to bed mad. I felt so light when I was laughing with you."

I nod. Light is how I felt too.

"I don't know how you feel about that," she says to me.

I look at her. I gulp. "The same." I say. Any more words and I may have choked.

A few minutes later, we go home.

On our way, we retrace the steps we'd taken during the day.

"You have no idea how close I came to slugging you when you told me that Scott's new girlfriend's bra was stuck in his pants when he left the movie theater," says Alexa. "Although it would serve him right, the big goof."

"Those pancakes you made were awesome," says Phil, who's dejection at not being the hypnotist he thought he was is offset by the memory of Alexa calling him hot twice.

We're all laughing together, fighting for space on the sidewalk so we can walk three abreast. "The best part," I say, "was when you said Phil was punctual. That killed me. I'll laugh at that forever."

Alexa agrees with me.

So does Phil.

I'm lying, though. This is the best part, right here. Right now. This is the part I want to remember forever.

Don Trembath is the best-selling author of several books for juveniles and young adults including *Rooster*, *The Tuesday Café* and the popular *Black Belt* Series. Don lives in Morinville, Alberta.